AF594312

Birdies Eternal

Birdies Eternal

A Treasury of Timeless Tales and Tips from HARRY VARDON, Golf's Great Champion for the Ages

Harry Vardon

TowleHouse Publishing
Nashville, Tennessee

TowleHouse books are distributed by National Book Network (NBN), 4720 Boston Way, Lanham, Maryland 20706.

Cataloging-in-Publication data is available.
ISBN: 1-931249-00-8

Cover design by Gore Studio, Inc.
Page design by Mike Towle

Printed in the United States of America
1 2 3 4 5 6 — 05 04 03 02 01

Contents

Introduction

About a hundred years ago Harry Vardon was the best golfer in the world, a six-time British Open champion from Jersey, an island in the English Channel. He came over to the United States in 1900 with much acclaim, and he even won that year's U.S. Open at Chicago Golf Club. It wasn't like Vardon was merely the biggest fish in a small pond. Although American golf was in its infancy at the turn of the century (nineteenth to twentieth), golf in some parts of Europe was huge, with dozens and even hundreds of crack golfers competing against each other in first-class tournaments from which legends were made and then revered.

In Vardon's heyday, there was a triumvirate of great golfers every bit as skilled and marveled as the more recent acclaimed trio of Jack Nicklaus, Arnold Palmer, and Gary Player—or Greg Norman, Nick Faldo, and Seve Ballesteros if

you want to bring it one generation closer to the present. Vardon's chief rivals circa 1900 were James Braid and J. H. Taylor, who between them won a total of sixteen British Opens; this at a time when the British Open was *the* Open, a true worldwide championship acknowledged as such. Golf had already been around for hundreds of years in locales such as Scotland, and Vardon, Braid, and Taylor were merely the latest in a long lineage of golfers that graced Great Britain.

Vardon passed away in the 1930s, and he left behind a multifaceted legacy that remains a prominent part of golf today. The so-called Vardon grip, the style of gripping the club with overlapped hands instead of interlocked, remains a popular foundation to the golf swing. His name also adorns the trophy given annually to the PGA Tour pro with the lowest scoring average in tour events, both for the American tour and the European version.

Vardon toiled at the game long before golf was ever televised and was in his championship prime well in advance of when golf hit the front page of sports sections in America. But he was a true expert and connoisseur of the game as reflected in the more than half-dozen books he authored over a twenty-five-year period. His wit and wisdom, as well as his ease in explaining the golf swing and golf strategy, are evident in all his works. Incredibly, much of what he said and wrote eighty, ninety, or a hundred years ago remains as topical and insightful today as it did in his era. This book is a snapshot representation of Harry Vardon at his literary best and offers timeless tips and instruction that will help golfers in ways t no other golf book can. A tip of the hat goes to the United States Golf Association and Dr. Rand Jerris for going the extra mile in granting access to Vardon's works.

Herry Vardon. (Dale Concannon Collection at the Phil Sheldon Golf Library)

Birdies Eternal

1

The Game

Golf is a strange game: It enchants and aggravates, it flatters and disappoints, it rears up to the player to believe in his efficiency and then lets him down with a crash. It is a kind of kaleidoscope interrupted at intervals by nightmares. It no sooner elevates its devotee than it dispirits him; it no sooner dispirits him than it elates him. That is the secret of its seductiveness, and at the back of it all is an illimitable vista of hope.

A great deal of unnecessarily bad golf is played in this world. The people who go on playing it, year in and year out, with unquenchable hope and enthusiasm, constitute the game's mainstay, for their zeal is complete, and zeal that remains unabated in the face of long-sustained adversity is the most powerful constituent in the whole fabric of a prosperous pastime.

There is no reason why a physically sound individual, who takes up the game before old age with the determination to succeed at it, should fail to develop form justifying a tolerably low handicap—say, five or six.

Golf, for all the appearance of tame tranquility that it is apt to present to the uninitiated mind, provides a more searching test of nerve and temperament than any other game in the world.

In order to be a champion, a person must have a good deal of sensitiveness in his nervous system. The man of sluggish disposition, the player with a truly "phlegmatic temperament" (that phrase which is so often used approvingly in regard to the individual who remains outwardly calm in a crisis) would not be likely to rise to greatness on the links.

Of all games, golf is the one that comes nearest to being an art. It is pursued with deliberation and method; its inspirations are the player's own creation, since he is never called upon to strike a moving ball the action of which has been influenced by his rival. It demands the greatest delicacy and accuracy of touch, as well as, in many circumstances, the power to hit hard. An art requires a sensitive nervous system, and in golf the difference between two sections of first-class players to whom I have referred is, presumably, that one who can keep his nerves under control during the most trying period and the other cannot.

On a recent summer's afternoon, when the ball had been soaring and bounding from well-hit tee shots over some three hundred yards of country, when the course, even as we finished at five o'clock, seemed to be alive at every point with folk in full enjoyment of this wonderful game, I fell to thinking in a more or less haphazard way of the developments which had taken place in golf during the time that I had known it. And I could not help marveling; I could not help rejoicing at having been lucky enough to live through what had been surely the most crowded age that . . . pastime knew.

Golf is a pastime that compels a person to want to do better than ever he has done in the past. Its nature is to open up wonderful possibilities and generate inexhaustible hope. And so the player is always believing in his power to improve.

Amongst games, golf has a nature peculiarly its own, and in no respect is its distinctiveness more marked than the circumstance that it allows its devotees practically a free hand in the choice of implements, the ball, and the extent and general characteristics of the playing ground. Golf, then, is apt to alter considerably as the seasons come and go. It is a game in which the sentiment of liberty holds sway.

FAR MORE THAN ANY OTHER GAME DOES GOLF LEND ITSELF TO THE PROVISION OF STRANGE INCIDENTS AND EXCITING LITTLE ADVENTURES. IT IS PLAYED IN A SETTING OF NATURE; ITS HOME IS ON THE OPEN MOORLAND OR THE ROLLING LINKS BY THE SEA; THERE IS MUCH IN IT THAT APPEALS TO THE PRIMEVAL INSTINCTS OF MAN BECAUSE OF THE UNRESTRAINT OF ITS ENVIRONMENT.

I HESITATE TO BELIEVE THE STORY WHICH ANDREW KIRKALDY TOLD US WHEN HE CAME BACK FROM MEXICO, THAT IT WAS A COMMON THING TO BE CONFRONTED AT A LONELY PART OF THE COURSE BY A BANDIT WHO SUDDENLY EMERGED FROM A WOOD AND WITH THE COMMAND, SUPPORTED BY A SIX-SHOOTER: "HANDS UP! YOUR MONEY OR YOUR LIFE!" PROCEED TO ROB THE MATCH OF ALL ITS VALUABLES. BUT WE HAVE ALL READ WITH BATED BREATH OF THE PERILS WHICH ARE ENCOUNTERED BY ENTHUSIASTS IN SOME COUNTRIES, WHERE SAVAGE BEASTS OF THE FOREST ARE AMONG "THE AGENCIES OUTSIDE THE MATCH," AND DEATH-DEALING SNAKES ARE SAID SOMETIMES TO BE FOUND COILED UP IN THE HOLES. I AM GLAD TO SAY I HAVE NOT YET BEEN SUBJECTED TO THE TRIAL OF PLAYING A GAME AMID SUCH DISTRACTIONS, BUT IN ENGLAND I HAVE HAD ONE ENGAGEMENT WITH AN ANIMAL WHICH I SHALL NOT READILY FORGET, AND WHICH GAVE ME A VERY ANXIOUS FIVE MINUTES.

THE EPISODE OCCURRED WHEN I WAS A PROFESSIONAL TO THE BURY CLUB, LANCASHIRE, SOMETHING LIKE THIRTY YEARS AGO. IN THOSE DAYS, GOLF EKED OUT A RATHER PRECARIOUS EXISTENCE IN ENGLAND. THE LANDLORD OF THE GROUND ON WHICH OUR COURSE WAS SITUATED HAD NO RESPECT AT ALL FOR THE PEOPLE WHO CAME TO HIT A BALL ABOUT HIS ESTATE. WE WERE THERE ON SUFFERANCE, AND ONE OF THE TROUBLES THAT WE HAD TO ENDURE WAS THAT HE INSISTED ON PUTTING HIS PRIZE BULLS TO GRAZE ON THE COURSE. THEY WERE A FINE COLLECTION OF ANIMALS, AND ONE—A WHITE BULL—HAD SECURED FOR HIM MANY PRIZES, BUT THEY MADE A ROUND OF GOLF A RISKY PROCEEDING, AND THERE WERE MANY PLAYERS WHO WOULD NOT VENTURE SO FAR AS THE FIRST TEE WHEN THESE BOVINE HAZARDS WERE IN EVIDENCE.

THE WHITE BULL WAS PARTICULARLY ILL-DISPOSED TOWARDS US. OFTEN IT SENT US SCUTTLING TO PLACES OF SAFETY WHEN, JUST AS WE WERE PREPARING TO ACCOMPLISH A CRITICAL SHOT, WE SAW IT GALLOPING TOWARDS US, WITH EYES ABLAZE AND TAIL WHIRLING FEROCIOUSLY IN THE AIR. I HAD TO MAKE SEVERAL HASTY AND UNDIGNIFIED FLIGHTS IN CONSEQUENCE OF ITS UNRULINESS; BUT WHENEVER ANYBODY COMPLAINED TO THE LANDLORD ABOUT ITS BEHAVIOR HE INVARIABLY SAID: "YOU SHOULDN'T TEASE HIM. HE WOULD BE ALL RIGHT IF YOU'D LEAVE HIM ALONE."

ONE DAY I DECIDED UPON WHAT SEEMED TO ME TO BE A FINE PLAN. OUR PUTTING GREENS WERE SURROUNDED BY WIRE, SO AS TO PROTECT THEM FROM INVASION BY ANIMALS. AFTER ABOUT THE FIFTIETH OF MY RETREATS FROM THE WHITE BULL, I TOLD THE OWNER THAT IF IT EVER WENT FOR ME AGAIN I SHOULD ENTER INTO ONE OF THOSE PROTECTED AREAS, WAIT FOR THE ANIMAL TO COME UP TO THE WIRE, AND THEN STICK IT IN A VITAL PART WITH THE FLAG-PIN WHICH WAS IN THE HOLE. THE FLAG-PIN STRUCK ME AS A SPLENDID IDEA; ALREADY I SAW MYSELF IN THE RÔLE OF TOREADOR.

"DON'T TEASE THE THING," HE SAID AGAIN, "AND YOU WON'T HAVE ANY TROUBLE WITH IT."

NOT LONG AFTERWARDS, I WAS INSPECTING THE COURSE IN CONNECTION WITH THE WORK OF ITS UPKEEP, WHEN I SAW THE BULL APPROACHING ME IN ITS USUAL TRUCULENT MOOD. IT WAS FAST GATHERING PACE, SO I MADE A DASH FOR A PUTTING GREEN, LEAPED OVER THE WIRE, SEIZED THE FLAG-PIN, AND RETURNED TO THE FORTIFICATION TO CARRY OUT MY STERN RESOLVE. ON CAME THE BULL UNTIL IT REACHED THE BULWARK—AND THEN, TO MY HORRIFIED ASTONISHMENT, IT CALMLY PUT ITS FEET OVER THE WIRE AND WAS IN THE ENCLOSURE WITH ME.

I JUMPED OUT AGAIN, AND FORTUNATELY RETAINED SUFFICIENT SELF-POSSESSION TO REALIZE THAT IN THE OPEN FIELD IT WOULD BE NO USE TRYING TO OUTPACE THE ANIMAL. I STARTED TO RUN AROUND THE WIRE ON THE OUTSIDE, WHEREUPON THE BULL FOLLOWED ME ON THE INSIDE. ROUND AND ROUND WE WENT, I KNOW NOT HOW MANY TIMES.

EVERY NOW AND AGAIN THE ENEMY MADE A DASH AT ME, BUT THE WIRE KEPT HIM BACK, AND LUCKILY FOR ME IT NEVER OCCURRED TO HIM TO COME OUT AS HE HAD ENTERED. I REALIZED, HOWEVER, THAT IF I RAN AWAY OR STOPPED STILL, HE WOULD BE OVER IN AN INSTANT.

WHICH OF US WOULD HAVE COLLAPSED FIRST I DO NOT KNOW. THE QUESTION WAS NEVER PUT TO THE TEST, THANKS TO THE PROVIDENTIAL INTERVENTION OF A MUFFIN-MAN. ON A ROAD ABOUT A HUNDRED YARDS AWAY THIS MUFFIN-MAN APPROACHED, RINGING HIS BELL. DIRECTLY THE BULL HEARD THE TINKLE, IT SET OFF PELL-MELL IN THE DIRECTION OF MY INNOCENT DELIVERER. A HEDGE ON THE FRINGE OF THE THOROUGHFARE BARRED ITS PROGRESS, AND MEANWHILE I FLED TO A PLACE OF SAFETY.

THERE WAS A RATHER INTERESTING SEQUEL TO THIS INCIDENT. ONE DAY I WAS RELAYING A TEEING GROUND CLOSE TO THE FOWL-HOUSE WHICH GRACED THE COURSE. IN THE MIDST OF

MY WORK MY ATTENTION WAS SUDDENLY DIVERTED BY THE SPECTACLE OF THE WHITE BULL CHASING ITS OWNER. HE WAS RUNNING LIKE A MADMAN, AND EVIDENTLY IN A STATE OF PANIC, AND IN HIS DESPERATION HE DASHED INTO THE MIDDLE OF THE DUCK-POND NEAR THE FOWL-HOUSE, WHERE HE STOOD ALMOST UP TO HIS NECK IN WATER. I HAVE TO CONFESS AT THIS MOMENT I WAS SO UNSYMPATHETIC AS TO SHOUT: "YOU SHOULDN'T TEASE THE ANIMAL. HE'D BE ALL RIGHT IF YOU'D LEAVE HIM ALONE."

THE BULL RUSHED UP TO THE EDGE OF THE POND, WHERE HE STOOD LASHING HIS TAIL ANGRILY AND GLARING FIERCELY AT HIS MASTER. THEN FOLLOWED ONE OF THE PLUCKIEST DEEDS I HAVE EVER SEEN DONE BY A BOY. THE LANDLORD'S SON, A YOUTH OF ABOUT TEN, SEIZED THE ANIMAL BY THE TAIL, AND TRIED TO PULL HIM AWAY. THE BULL TURNED AROUND SEVERAL TIMES IN SAVAGE ATTEMPTS TO GET AT THE BOY, BUT HE HELD ON LIKE GRIM DEATH. ALL OF AN INSTANT THE ANIMAL SET OFF AT TOP PACE FOR ITS SHED, DRAGGING ITS ASSAILANT AT ITS HEELS, AND A FEW MINUTES LATER IT WAS SAFELY INSIDE. THE OWNER WAS SO ENRAGED THAT HE FOLLOWED IT IN AND KILLED IT BY STICKING IT WITH A FOUR-PRONGED [PITCH]FORK, AND THAT WAS THE END OF OUR TROUBLES WITH THE WHITE BULL OF BURY.

I used to know a clergyman who suffered unspeakable agony in his effort to control his feelings when he hit a ball into a bunker. In the graphic words of his caddie: "Big blue pimples would come out on his face, and you'd think he was going to have a fit." In these crises, he always snatched from an inside pocket a prayer book and scurried forward reading it until gradually his rage subsided, and he found himself capable of tackling the situation with a tranquil mind. It must be for everybody to decide how he can best placate himself in such emergencies.

Many amateurs fail to attain that degree of success which is within their reach for the simple reason that they do not reflect sufficiently upon the possibilities, especially where small points are concerned.

No true golfer is satisfied with a little of the game, if there is no substantial reason why he should not have much of it.

There will be duffings and toppings and slicings, but one day there will be a long straight drive right away down the course, and the tyro will be told that the professional himself could not have done it better. This is one of the most pleasurable moments in life.

It is only when a man has everything to lose and nothing to gain that he should become uneasy about his game.

Unless by pure accident, no good ever comes of a bad stroke.

There are fewer certainties in golf than in any other game, and dogged pluck is rarely so well rewarded as on the links.

I like to see a lady go out on the golf links in whatever costume she thinks fit to wear for her own comfort and good play, and generally do as she likes, as if there were nothing but Nature and a little white ball and the hole with the flag in it in all the world.

Imagination has a practical value in golf.

GOLF SHOTS SOMETIMES MEET WITH STRANGE FATES, AND I THINK THE QUEEREST I EVER PLAYED WAS AT ST. ANDREWS. I WAS DOING A GOOD ROUND UNTIL I CAME TO THE LAST HOLE. ON THE RIGHT OF THE COURSE AT THIS HOLE IS A ROW OF HOUSES, BUT THEY ARE SO FAR AWAY AS USUALLY TO BE SAFE. ON THIS OCCASION, HOWEVER, I IMPARTED SO TERRIFIC A SLICE TO MY BALL THAT IT LANDED ON TOP OF ONE OF THE BUILDINGS, BOUNCED DOWN, AND FINISHED ITS CAREER IN A DRAINPIPE.

AN ERRANT SHOT THAT HAD A HAPPIER ENDING WAS ONE WHICH I SAW PLAYED AT GANTON, IN YORKSHIRE, WHEN I WAS A PROFESSIONAL THERE. A GOLFER HIT A TEE SHOT WHICH STRUCK A CADDIE ON THE HEAD, WHENCE IT REBOUNDED ONTO THE CLUB-HOUSE, AND FROM THERE ONTO THE GREEN, WHERE IT LAY WITHIN EASY HOLING DISTANCE. WE ALL EXPECTED TO SEE THE CADDIE DROP IN A STUNNED CONDITION, BUT HE STOOD HIS GROUND AND, ON BEING PRESENTED WITH A SOVEREIGN BY THE RELIEVED PLAYER, HE SAID WITH A GRIN, "HAVE ANOTHER TRY!"

On British courses a good many ponds have been either drained and converted into bunkers or filled up during recent years. A desire to avert unnecessary loss of balls may have been largely responsible for this tendency, but it is certain that in many places the reason is to be found in the weird enchantment which water exercises on the shots of a considerable proportion of the members.

No, deeply as I grieve at the passing of the gutty, I do not see how it is to be reinstated, even to the limited extent of its being made a standard ball for championships. The rubber-core is established, and nothing can shift it without creating fresh embarrassment. It has had one useful effect. I believe that it has been responsible to some extent for the enormously increased popularity of golf. By making the game easier, it has flattered many people into the belief that they are better players than is the case, and that they can master the finer points of the pastime in a period which, in due course, they discover to be hopelessly insufficient for the purpose.

Wherever I have gone, the same evidence of a falling-off in the intrinsic quality of the golf has been manifest, and it is attributable to the influence of the rubber-cored ball. For one thing, players have become careless. The miss is sometimes better than the hit; and everybody is aware of that fact. There was wisdom in the remark of one of my opponents who had topped his mashie stroke to within holing distance: "Any old shot will do nowadays." All too often it will do remarkably well. In the time of the gutty, a player knew that if he perpetrated a bad stroke, he would be punished. He would be short, or, if his ball reached a bunker, it would not jump the hazard. The knowledge that there was no mercy for those who erred impelled him to be careful. There was only one way to play every shot; it has to be played properly.

Outdoor life in Great Britain belongs as much to women as to men, but from my observation the American woman gets too little of it. It is my hope to see golf prove the lure to draw her out into the sunlight and pure air of the green fields. It will help to give her the ever-present enjoyment which comes from a calm mind in a healthy, vigorous body.

A number of years elapsed between my last two visits to the United States, and between those dates the strides that have been made in the construction of courses, the number of players, the building of clubs, and the general development of the game have been to me extraordinary.

This rapid growth has brought with it many of the evils which attend an almost too-rapid expansion of any line of human endeavor, and one of these evils is the lack of competent, expert instruction to the beginner in golf . . .

As a result, thousands of players take up the game in a most haphazard manner. They select their clubs with no guidance whatsoever, and they begin their play with no knowledge of the rudiments of the game, and thus their development is retarded, and they form habits of play which the most expert instruction finds almost impossible to correct.

IN SOME RESPECTS THE MOST TRYING ORDEAL THROUGH WHICH I EVER PASSED WAS PRESENTED IN A SPORTING GOODS STORE IN BOSTON DURING MY FIRST TOUR IN THE STATES OVER TWENTY YEARS AGO . . . THE GOLF BOOM IN AMERICA WAS JUST BEGINNING TO BE SOMETHING REALLY BIG, AND THE MANAGER OF THE STORE CONCEIVED THE IDEA OF MY PLAYING SHOTS INTO A NET ERECTED IN ONE OF THE SHOWROOMS. HE OFFERED ME SO HANDSOME A REWARD FOR THE EXHIBITION THAT NO SANE PROFESSIONAL WOULD HAVE REFUSED IT, AND ON THE APPOINTED DAY I DULY PUT IN AN APPEARANCE, READY TO BEGIN PROCEEDINGS AS ARRANGED AT HALF-PAST NINE IN THE MORNING. THE PLAN WAS THAT I SHOULD HIT SHOTS INTO THE NET FOR HALF-AN-HOUR, REST FOR HALF-AN-HOUR, BEGIN AGAIN, AND SO ON TILL FIVE O'CLOCK CAME.

THE ROOM WAS PACKED (THERE MUST HAVE BEEN SOME HUNDREDS OF PEOPLE PRESENT AT THE TIME), AND AT THE END OF THE FIRST THIRTY MINUTES I RETIRED IN ACCORDANCE WITH THE PROGRAM.

GREATLY TO MY ASTONISHMENT THE SPECTATORS BROKE INTO THUNDEROUS APPLAUSE; THEY CLAPPED, CHEERED, AND THUMPED THEIR STICKS AND UMBRELLAS ON THE FLOOR WITH SUCH PERSISTENCY THAT I HAD TO RETURN.

Harry Vardon and James Braid, two of their era's greatest champions. (Dale Concannon Collection at Phil Sheldon Golf Picture Library)

AFTER ANOTHER SPELL OF ABOUT HALF-AN-HOUR I AGAIN RETIRED, BUT THE APPRECIATION WAS AS EMBARRASSING AS IN THE FORMER INTERVAL, AND I WAS OBLIGED TO RESUME IMMEDIATELY.

PEOPLE WERE CONSTANTLY COMING AND GOING, BUT THE FRESH ARRIVALS SEEMED TO BE AS SATISFIED AS THEIR PREDECESSORS, AND I DID NOT OBTAIN FIVE MINUTES' REST. WHAT ANYBODY CAN HAVE SEEN IN THE PERFORMANCE I DO NOT KNOW—DRIVING A BALL INTO A NET IS HARDLY THRILLING—BUT I HAD TO DO IT ALL DAY . . .

AT ABOUT FOUR O'CLOCK I FELT THAT I HAD HAD ENOUGH OF IT. I MADE MY CUSTOMARY EXIT; THE APPLAUSE RESTARTED, BUT ONCE I WAS OUT OF THE SHOWROOM I FLED FROM THE BUILDING. NOBODY COULD HAVE CONTINUED THE GAME ANY LONGER.

THE MANAGER TOLD ME AFTERWARDS THAT DURING THE DAY THEY SOLD EVERY CLUB IN THE SHOP. THAT WILL GIVE YOU SOME IDEA OF THE ENTHUSIASM WITH WHICH GOLF WAS TAKEN UP IN THE EARLY DAYS OF ITS BOOM IN AMERICA.

IN 1899 I WENT TO NORTH BERWICK TO PLAY THE FIRST HALF OF MY MATCH WITH WILLIE PARK—THE EVENT WHICH I REGARDED AS THE MOST IMPORTANT OF MY GOLFING CAREER. IT WAS SO BECAUSE IT PROVOKED DISCUSSION FOR NEARLY A YEAR BEFORE IT TOOK PLACE (WE WERE A LONG TIME COMING TO TERMS), AND I DO NOT THINK THAT TWO MEN EVER EMBARKED ON A CONTEST WITH A MORE DESPERATE DESIRE TO WIN.

ON THE EVENING BEFORE THE BEGINNING OF OUR MATCH, I WENT FOR A WALK WITH MY BROTHER TOM. SUDDENLY "BIG" CRAWFORD [ONE OF THAT ERA'S MOST FAMOUS NORTH BERWICK CADDIES] APPEARED ROUND A CORNER, AND LIKE A FLASH HE HURLED A HUGE HORSESHOE AT ME.

IF I HAD NOT DODGED IT, IT WOULD HAVE STRUCK ME ON THE HEAD, AND AT THE PACE AT WHICH IT WAS TRAVELING IT WOULD VERY NEARLY HAVE BRAINED ME. TRUTH TO TELL, I DID NOT ALTOGETHER APPRECIATE THIS METHOD OF DELIVERING GOOD FORTUNE, BUT IT WAS IMPOSSIBLE TO DO OTHER THAN LAUGH WHEN HE EXPLAINED THAT HE HAD PUT EVERY PENNY HE POSSESSED ON ME AND WAS DETERMINED TO BRING ME LUCK.

(Vardon finished the first half of the match the next day two up on Park and later completed his victory by a comfortable margin, 11&10.)

Is there not the famous case of the Anglo-Indian sportsman, one of the mightiest of hunters, who feared nothing like the hole when it lay so near to him that his tears of agony might almost have fallen into it? It was this man who declared, "I have encountered all the manifold perils of the jungle, I have tracked the huge elephant to his destruction, and I have stood eye to eye with the man-eating tiger. And never once have I trembled until I came to a short putt." Yet with such facts as these before us, some people still wonder wherein lies the fascination of golf.

2
Clubs and Equipment

Old Names for Golf Clubs and Their Approximate Modern-Day Equivalents

(Ed. note: Notice some apparant overlap, but similar clubs used for different purposes)

Driver = driver

Brassie = two-wood

Spoon = three-wood

Baffy = four-wood

Wood Cleek = five-wood

Cleek = two-iron

Driving Iron = one- or two-iron

Mid Iron = two-iron

Jigger = four-iron (another source said eight-iron . . . go figure)

Mashie = five-iron

Mashie-Niblick = seven-iron

Niblick = nine-iron

The absolute beginner cannot do better than borrow an old club from a professional and discover his natural stance, length of swing, and other individualities before he proceeds to purchase a set of implements. The professional will be able to tell him at the end of ten minutes what sort of tools will suit him best.

In the case of a golfer of some experience, instinct is the best adviser in the choice of a club. As you take the creation in your hands, you can generally tell at once whether it is just the thing that you have been wanting for a long while . . . Looks are often deceiving; they ought to have no influence in the making of the final selection. A club that is by no means pleasing to the eye is sometimes found to be the best of the bunch when the prospector tries the "feel" of it.

I am satisfied that nine out of ten experts will agree that for a beginner, (the) first clubs should be a brassie, a mid iron, a mashie, a putter, and a niblick. It is almost impossible to get around the course without having an urgent need for each of these clubs.

More than once I have heard amateurs say, "No wonder professionals play so well, they always pick the best clubs." It is not so much a matter of choosing the best—everybody does that—as of selecting those which are in the nature of brothers. The golfer needs what I might call a family group of clubs. The "lie"—that is, the inclination of the club as it is held on the ground in the ordinary position for striking—should be similar in his set in the sense that the full extent of the sole of each club should be capable of resting naturally on the ground when the player is standing ready for the shot.

I am all for the golfer making the game as easy as he can for himself by the judicious selection of clubs.

There is a tremendous difference in golf clubs. This difference lies essentially in the character of the material used as well as the workmanship employed to produce it. A good golf club consists largely of a good shaft. This is the one thing that must be right. It is comparatively easy to make a reasonably good head, but it is one of the most difficult and mysterious of sciences to produce a good golf shaft.

Expressing the importance of the shaft mathematically, I should say that the shaft is nine-tenths of the club. Of course, a head having the wrong lie and loft will detract greatly from the efficiency of the club, but these defects are easily obviated by a little care.

The lie is represented by the angle formed by the line of the shaft with the true sole of the head of the club . . . The loft of the club is the angle of the striking face with the sole of the club. This is very important and should be watched very carefully. A driver face is much more nearly the perpendicular than any other wooden club.

The third point to be noted with great care is to see whether the wood head has any slice or pull to it. If the face of the wood head is perfectly true, then the face of the club will be on a line parallel with the line of the shaft.

When the line of the face angles from the shaft outward to the left, the club has a hook; when to the right, a slice.

It is customary to allow a very slight hook to the face of the club because of the almost universal tendency of the player to slice.

Without question, what are commonly termed the balance and spring of a golf club are the most difficult points about it to describe. In fact, only the expert can understand thoroughly, although the amateur herself, after a long experience, learns to tell whether a club feels right in her hands. This may be due either to the spring in the shaft, to the balance of the club, or a combination of the two. The club should be well balanced and should have just enough spring in the shaft to give to the player the sense of power and confidence which she needs in playing the game.

Coming now to the iron heads, we find a much greater variety of lie and loft and shape than can possibly be represented in the wooden heads. The number of different models of iron heads seems almost infinite. The ingenuity and imagination of golfers for years has devoted itself to the fashioning of almost every conceivable shape of blade and neck, but when all is said and done, the great players depart very little from the plain lines which common sense and good judgment dictate.

~

The style of scoring or face marking is unimportant, but the weight, lie, and loft are the elements which should enter into a reliable and trustworthy iron head. The depth of the blade and distribution of the weight are both factors, especially the latter. The weight of an iron head should be so located that the center of impact is near the middle of the face of the blade. The most of the weight of the head should be in the blade and only enough in the socket to insure a right connection with the shaft.

~

The third and last portion of a golf club is the grip. It should be of the proper size to fit the hand, the average size for women being about three-fourths of an inch in diameter. A cushion effect is imparted by a layer of cloth next to the . . . handle. Several kinds of leather are used for grips. Sheepskins and other leathers have been employed, some substance generally being used on the grip to make it sticky and less liable to slip.

Split calf and sheepskin make a very low-priced but satisfactory grip, and the rubber grip is still more reasonable in cost . . . Another grip which has considerable popularity is a rough leather called "Gold Cape." Some professionals in the States seem to prefer that to the smooth calf. This grip is not rendered slippery by being wet as is the case with the smooth calf.

The grip should be fastened tightly to the club and ought to be from eleven inches to twelve inches in length. It ought to taper very slightly from the top of the grip to its lower end, but this taper should be hardly perceptible.

Vardon was consistently plagued by ill health during his career, and he even spent some time in a sanatorium. He was nicknamed "Greyhound" by fellow pro Andrew Kirkaldy for his ability to race through in the final stages of a tournament. (Dale Concannon Collection at Phil Sheldon Golf Picture Library)

Be sure that the grip is put on uniformly and smoothly. Specially formed grips for the purpose of forcing the player to always hold the club in exactly the same manner are not advisable. As you progress in the game, you will realize that the hand cannot always occupy exactly the same place in order to execute the same stroke.

I recommend thin grips for all clubs. I tried thick grips for a short time; but did not get on at all well with what I called my "cricket bats." They were a desperate remedy that proved worse than the disease.

Never use thick handle grips. They place weight at the wrong end of the club.

A player whose muscles are loose and permit of a very quick, full, free swing, should use a stiffer shaft in her brassie [driving club] than one who uses a short restricted swing because of her weight or slow muscular habits.

(The mid iron) is chiefly used for long approach strokes where the distance is too great for the mashie and not enough for the brassie. The mid iron is also used where the lie is too low for the brassie or where not lying too badly in rough grass and yet as much distance as possible is desired. The iron head will cut through the turf and soil without greatly diminishing its force on the ball where a wood club would be perceptibly slow.

(The mashie) is also shorter than the mid iron because great accuracy in both distance and direction is required in approach strokes. It is the logical approach iron, and a good approach may save at least one stroke and perhaps two. Of all the clubs in your bag, you should treasure your mashie most. Be exceedingly careful in your selection of it. Be sure that the loft is right, that the lie is correct, and be careful to have a stiff, rigid shaft.

The niblick is the heaviest in the set. The lie is fairly upright and the face has more loft than any other club in the bag . . . The shaft is the most rigid of any and should be larger than any other iron shaft because the club is played in long grass, sand, and sometimes around rocks and other obstacles, and the strain on the club may be very considerable. It is used almost exclusively as the means of getting out of sand bunkers, roads, rough places, and extremely heavy grass.

You must suit your own style with reference to the lie of your putter, whether upright, medium, or flat . . . I prefer the straight-face putter, but that, too, is merely a matter of taste. Use the putter in which you have the greatest confidence. Do not hesitate to try new putters, but if you are to begin sensibly, select a straight-face, straight-necked putter, and learn your stroke with that.

Suppose you are not normal [in physical development or muscular habits]. Instead, through some injury or sickness you are weak, and you cannot summon and maintain that spontaneous action of all the muscles . . . In such a case, your clubs should be lighter and shorter than the normal.

The driver [one-wood] is the first club to master after you have become familiar with the five already in your bag. This should be exactly of the same weight and length as your brassie.

In choosing clubs, never take a club that seems too heavy to swing accurately and within your control.

The brassie shaft should be stiffer than that of the driver because the head of the brassie often goes through grass or touches the turf.

~

The deeply grooved face type of clubs used to increase the backspin on approach strokes is worthy of comment here. These clubs are variously named backspin, shurstop, stop-um, dropded, etc., to indicate the effect of their use. They consist of mashies, mashie-niblicks, and sometimes niblicks with heavily corrugated faces in place of the usual line or dot scoring. The ribs of the corrugations catch the surface of the ball at the moment of impact and impart a tremendous reverse whirl like that of the draw shot in billiards . . . I strongly recommend these clubs to all golfers.

~

There are heretics who . . . may come up for the humble judgment of a conscientious golfer. They are the people who use nothing but irons—even from the tee. They are not only unorthodox and blind to their own interests; they are faint-hearted. They think that they cannot master wooden clubs, and they have not the courage to make a determined effort to do so. They seek to evade the difficulties of the game by accomplishing their tee shots with a driving mashie or kindred instrument. They will never make good players, and they will never know the full joy of the links.

The good golfer loves his clubs and takes a great and justifiable pride in them.

I like to see a golfer play with bright irons, and shafts that give evidence of tender and affectionate care.

If I were a left-handed player, I would make it a point to have clubs specially made for me.

Once on the green, the putter is the sole club to be used to hole the ball.

3
The Swing

A golfer's swing is often made for good or ill in the first week of his experience.

Perfect confidence and a calm mind are necessary for the success of every stroke.

The golf swing is different from anything else in sport. It deserves to be called an art.

Let the neophyte, or the player who fears that he is an incurably bad golfer, resolve to master first of all the way of executing a shot off the tee with his brassie. This is the easiest full shot in the realm of golf, and the accomplishment of it always affords a thrill of pleasure and encouragement.

The club is held so that the two thumbs rest on the shaft, and, with the forefingers, form *V*s. The right hand, instead of being under the shaft, is brought round, and the back of that hand faces away from the line of play. The back of the left hand looks towards the line of play.

Here, then, we have the hands nicely balanced—the backs of the hands facing in opposite directions, and the thumbs and forefingers formed into *V*s with their apex uppermost. This is a sound grip so long as you remember to make the hands meet on the shaft. They must not be apart, even to the extent of the tiniest fraction of an inch.

I do not believe there is such a thing as a master arm in the real golf swing. The two arms work as one, and as part of the entire mechanism of the body.

The stance must be easy and comfortable without undue stooping or any degree of stiffness.

Keeping the eye on the ball is important, and I do not suggest that anybody should forget it. But it is a secondary point. Keeping the head still is the prime essential.

When we are talking about keeping the eye on the ball, we do not mean the top of the ball. Your object is not to hit the top of the ball with the bottom of your club. For an ordinary stroke keep your attention fixed on the grass immediately behind the ball.

Vardon demonstrates the proper stance with a driver. He wrote: "The grip is all important, the one I advocate being the two V overlapping grip, formed by the thumb and forefingers . . . Weight evenly distributed on both legs; no stiffness of body." (From The Gist of Golf)

This is what Vardon looked like at the top of the driver swing. He wrote: "The left knee has continued its inward movement, while with the head kept perfectly still, the turn of the hips has been completed and the even distribution of the weight of the body maintained." (*From* The Gist of Golf)

When you are addressing the ball, and a conviction forces itself on your mind just before making the stroke that your stance or something else is radically wrong, do not be persuaded that it is best to get the stroke done with notwithstanding.

In addressing, always oppose to the ball that part of the face of the club with which you want to hit it.

[When teeing off] stand easily with a distinct sense of relaxation in the joints and muscles; if you tighten them during the up-swing through a determination to make a tremendously powerful shot, you are nearly sure to ruin the swing. You have nothing to hit till you come down.

The upward swing is made by two movements, one dovetailing so nicely into the other as to render the complete operation smooth and continuous. The first movement raises the club until its head is pointing upwards, the right hip screwing around the while. The second movement makes the elbows bend and lets the shaft fall into position behind the player's head . . . It is surprising how many golfers omit to perform the second movement in the swing. They raise the club stiffly and seem to consider that the highest point in the air which they can reach must represent the top of the swing, and that there is consequently no need to go back any farther. This half-swing . . . is an incomplete way of playing golf.

A long drive is not usually made purely by virtue of hard hitting.

"Slow back" is an excellent rule for the novice, and even for the advanced golfer. But by "slow back" I do not mean taking the implement back at snail's pace. Very often the maxim is dinned into the ears of the beginner with such assiduity that he worries himself almost to death in his endeavors to make the upward swing as slow as possible. That is as bad as too rapid a movement.

Go slowly back, but be quick on the ball. But do not swing back too slowly or you will lose control over your club. Gain speed gradually.

The stroke that sweeps the ball well away from the low tee is the most natural and perfect, and it follows that the ball, properly driven from this low tee, is the best of all . . . Another convincing argument in favor of the low tee is that it preserves a greater measure of similarity between the first shot and the second, helping to make the latter, with the brassie, almost a repetition of the first, and therefore simple and comparatively easy.

The desire to look up quickly is a natural one . . . there is anxiety to see immediately whether the ball is there. It will never be there unless we look at it long enough to strike it accurately. The head must be kept still with heroic determination until the follow-through is under way.

Seven golden rules of the golf drive:

1. Keep the head steady, and do not let the left heel turn outwards.
2. Grip firmest with the thumbs and forefingers.
3. Let the clubhead lead, the left wrist turning inwards, the arms following the clubhead, and the right hip screwing next.
4. Don't throw the arms forward as you start to come down . . . Rather throw them back, and let them come around in their own way from that point.
5. Let the movement of the right shoulder be steady and rhythmic.
6. Don't be afraid to hit hard.
7. Keep your head still until the club has struck the ball.

Sometimes one sees ladies golfing in large straw hats. They simply cannot be swinging properly, or they would knock their hats every time. At the top of the swing, the shaft should be so close to the player's head, without touching it, as to render impossible the wearing of a hat with a brim.

Grip [the club] a little tighter with the cleek or iron than with the driver or brassie . . . The slightly strengthened hold is desirable lest the implement turn in the hands at the moment of impact, a disaster which is apt to occur through the contact with the ground . . . [but] not so tight as to make blood run out of the knuckles.

If the feet are too far apart, it is impossible to pivot properly.

Do not forget to aim at a spot half an inch or even an inch behind the ball.

Judgment in the execution of approaches depends not upon deciding how hard to strike the ball. The real judgment consists of knowing just how far to take the club back.

(The mashie) seems about the most fickle of golfing tools; one day the best helpmate in the world, and on another occasion, the very deuce. The reason is that it is docile and obliging in the highest degree when it receives the proper treatment, but that any small error of mission or commission transforms it into a veritable demon of refractoriness.

Vardon in his younger days, circa 1900.(Dale Concannon Collection at Phil Sheldon Golf Picture Library)

The trait that distinguishes [the mashie shot] from every other stroke . . . is explainable in these words: It depends primarily upon the movement of the knees . . . We want to be very steady on our feet—almost as steady as if they were stuck to the ground.

For the ordinary golfer, I would seldom recommend more than a three-quarter swing with this particular (very particular) club, and there should be no pirouetting.

I am certain that forty of every fifty bad golfers owe their weakness with the mashie to this obsession in the matter of trying to shovel the ball into the air. They endeavor to carry it, so to speak, on the face of the club. That is impossible. What usually happens is that they strike the ground about three inches behind the ball, and a fearful foozle results . . . The club will produce the loft; the player need not bother about it.

A frequent cause of disaster, especially with iron clubs, is failure to ground the implement in a reasonable manner behind the ball.

~

Where most golfers make mistakes with the mashie is that they pivot too much on their feet, try to scoop the ball into the air instead of letting the loft of the club do the work for which it was built, and throw their weight forward at impact, at the same time raising their heads to see the result of the shot.

~

Amongst beginners, the most common fault is topping. That is curious because, to the person who has come to be capable of playing a good game, intentional topping is one of the most difficult feats in the realm of golf.

~

It is easy to fall into the habit of stretching the arms too much in the address in order to reach the ball; it is equally easy to avoid this straining by closing in a little on the ball.

~

IT WAS WITH A NIBLICK THAT I PLAYED THE BEST SHOT OF MY LIFE. THE OCCASION WAS A TOURNAMENT AT NORTHWOOD A FEW YEARS AGO. AT THE EIGHTEENTH HOLE, I SLICED MY SECOND SHOT. THE BALL LAY WITHIN ABOUT FOUR FEET OF THE CLUB-HOUSE, WHICH WAS NOW BETWEEN ME AND THE HOLE. AS YOU CAN IMAGINE, IT WAS A PRETTY BIG STYMIE, AND FOR A WHILE I HARDLY KNEW HOW TO TACKLE IT EXCEPT BY PLAYING OUT TO THE LEFT. AT LAST I DECIDED TO TRY AND CARRY THE BUILDING, AND REACH THE GREEN. THE PEOPLE ON THE VERANDA LOOKED RATHER SURPRISED WHEN I ASKED THEM TO STAND ASIDE IN CASE I SHOULD STRIKE THEM. THE VERANDA WAS PROTECTED BY WIRE NETTING, BUT I KNEW THAT I SHOULD HAVE TO HIT THE BALL HARD TO MAKE IT RISE ALMOST STRAIGHT INTO THE AIR UNTIL IT REACHED THE TOP OF THE CLUB-HOUSE, AND PUT ENOUGH SPIN ON IT TO CAUSE IT TO CARRY FORWARD THIRTY YARDS TO THE GREEN. IT IS NOT DIFFICULT TO GET A BALL TO RISE ALMOST PERPENDICULARLY, BUT TO MAKE IT START TO MOVE FORWARD WHEN IT IS THIRTY OR FORTY FEET FROM THE GROUND IS A DIFFERENT MATTER, AND I WAS AFRAID THAT, IF THE SHOT FAILED, I MIGHT SEND THE BALL THROUGH THE NETTING AND HIT SOMEBODY.

SO, SMILINGLY, THEY MOVED ASIDE. I USED A NIBLICK FOR THE SHOT. THE BALL FLEW UP, MOVING FORWARD NO MORE THAN A YARD UNTIL IT WAS ABOUT THIRTY FEET IN THE AIR; THEN IT WENT ON, CARRIED THE CLUB-HOUSE, AND STOPPED A YARD FROM THE HOLE. AND THEN I MISSED THE PUTT. THAT WAS A WRETCHED FINISH; BUT THE SHOT FROM DIRECTLY BEHIND THE BUILDING WAS THE BEST I EVER PLAYED, AND I AM FRANKLY AND BOYISHLY PROUD OF IT.

Occasions when the running-up approach offers the simplest means of reaching the vicinity of the hole are becoming more and more numerous . . . For this stroke it is desirable to stand more forward than for the ordinary mashie shot; the hands should be in front of the ball. This will tend to keep the ball low.

Vardon demonstrates the stance for a niblick (wedge) shot from a grass bunker. He wrote that the weight of the body must "be thrown rather more on the left leg." (From The Gist of Golf)

In taking the club back for the wedge shot out of the bunker, Vardon wrote: "The weight of the body has inclined even more on to the left leg. As this is one of the few forcing shots in golf, the club must be held very firmly." (From The Gist of Golf)

Slicing is the most unprofitable vice in the game . . . As a rule it is caused by swaying the body to the right during the upward swing (that is to say, not turning at the hips), or by perpetrating at the top of the swing, when the hips have screwed up properly, the common error of beginning to unwind at the hips before starting the club on its return journey.

Pulling is a curious phase of the game. In certain circumstance a little of it is excellent because it goes such a long way, or rather makes the ball go such a long way . . . It is often caused by a failure to turn the left wrist at the beginning of the upward swing so that the knuckles are visible . . . Another provocation of the pull is the fault of holding tighter with one hand than the other, and a third is turning the right hand over at the moment of impact.

There are some players who, while they nearly always strike the ball accurately and make it travel in a straight line, never succeed in driving far. The reason is that they are not making sufficient use of their arms. They are executing the stroke purely by the twist of the body, and not putting their arms into it.

THE "PUSH SHOT"—IMPARTING BACKSPIN:

Of first importance is the stance. The player must stand nearer to the ball than for the ordinary [iron] shot—he must close in on the ball to the extent of several inches—because his object is not to hit behind the ball and propel it high into the air, but to come down on the back of it by means of an upright swing which in itself necessitates this close stance to the ball.

The stance must be more forward, too, than for the ordinary shot. When you are in the position of address, with the club grounded just behind the ball, the hands must be an inch or two in front of the ball. Moreover, the vision must be directed, not on the turf just behind the ball, but on the back of the ball itself.

You see then the manner of striking the ball for which you are shaping. You are nearer to the ball than before, with the hands actually in front of it as you prepare for the shot, and you are going to perform something in the nature of a straight up-and-down swing—as nearly that as the arms will allow in comfort. You are not going to permit any waste or exuberance of the swing; you are going to take it to the top of a half or three-quarter swing by the shortest track you know that is consistent with rhythm and ease of movement, and come down on the back of the ball. You are going to "try and bang the back out of the ball," if one may so describe it. Even though you are hitting it forward, you must be conscious that you are beating it down rather than lifting it up, as is the case in the ordinary shot.

You ought not to be conscious that the hands in particular are doing a lot of hard work. Their function is to put the clubhead into the proper position for hitting the ball: not to do the hitting. They are to all intents and purposes a connecting link between the arms and the club—nothing more.

There is no earthly reason why so many golfers should have corns on their hands—the consequence of very tight gripping. Personally, I never have a corn on either of my hands except near the little finger of the left hand, and that is caused solely by the fact that I wear a ring on the finger mentioned.

After the impact, the clubhead should be allowed to follow the ball straight in the line of the flag as far as the arms will let it go, and then, having done everything that is possible, it swings itself out at the other side of the shoulders.

The arms should be kept fairly well in during the latter half of the downward swing, both elbows almost grazing the body. If they are properly attended to when the club is going up, there is much more likelihood of their coming down all right.

I don't believe in the long ball coming from the wrists . . . There is a kind of superstition that the elect among drivers get in some particular kind of "snap"—a momentary forward pushing movement—with their wrists at the time of impact, and that it is this wrist work at the critical period which gives the grand length to their drives, those extra twenty or thirty yards which make the stroke look so splendid, so uncommon, and which make the next shot so much easier. Generally speaking, the wrists when held firmly will take very good care of themselves.

Some players attempt to play their short approaches with their wrists as they have been told to do. These men are likely to remain at long handicaps for a long time.

Vardon drew a crowd wherever he went with a golf club in hand, whether it was a tournament in Europe or a sporting-goods store in Boston. Notice the natty attire of the spectators, proof certainly of a different era. (Dale Concannon Collection at Phil Sheldon Golf Picture Library)

Very rarely slice as a remedy against a cross wind. Either pull or nothing.

~

The commonest defect to be found with iron play is the failure to address the ball and play the stroke with the sole of the club laid evenly upon the ground from toe to heel.

~

[A] matter in which the philosophic golfer rises superior to his less favored brother when there is a bunker stroke to be played, is that he fully realizes that the bunker was placed there for the particular purpose of catching certain defective shots, and that the definite idea of its constructors was that the man who played such a shot should lose a stroke as penalty for doing so—every time . . . But the unphilosophic gentleman . . . feels that his bunkered stroke must be compensated for by the next one or never. What is the result? Recklessly, unscientifically, even ludicrously, he fires away at the ball in the bunker with a cleek or an iron or a mashie, striving his utmost to get length, when, with the frowning cliff of the bunker high in front of him and possibly even overhanging him, no length is possible.

When you have made a really wonderfully good shot—for you—bring yourself up sharply to find out exactly how you did it. Notice your stance, your grip, and try to remember the exact character of the swing that you made and precisely how you followed through. Then you will be able to do the same thing next time with great confidence.

4

Putting

Putting is, in a sense, a pastime distinct from golf. Half the secret of accomplishing it triumphantly lies, I suppose, in realizing that it is not very difficult.

Putting is so much a matter of confidence that I sometimes think that the average player ought to be better at it than the champion.

I believe seriously that every man has had a particular kind of putting method awarded to him by Nature, and when he putts exactly in this way he will do well, and when he departs from his natural system he will miss the long ones and the short ones, too.

Willie Park once said that "The man who can putt is a match for anybody," to which the obvious retort [is] that "The man who can approach has no need to be able to putt."

There is such a thing as trying too hard; it begets anxiety, which is usually fatal—especially in putting.

On a newly cut green there are stripes of different shades of green. The points of the grass give the deeper tints, and therefore the [mowing] machine has been coming towards you on the dark stripes, and along them you must putt harder than on the others.

Unquestionably the most important principle in putting is to keep the head and body absolutely still during the stroke. I know this from bitter experience.

The all-important matter is to light upon a method that gives you the feeling that you are going to succeed, and then to practice it.

It seems to me that golfers in considering their putts very often take too little pains to come to an accurate determination of the speed of the greens.

In all sincerity I express the opinion, after having undertaken three lengthy tours in the United States, that American golfers are better holers-out than British golfers. They are the cooler on the putting greens, and, after all, absence of anxiety is the chief essence of success.

When you are putting, your head should be as still as the dial of the clock; your body should be as stable as the case. Your arms, wrists, and club should constitute the pendulum. Then you will keep good time.

In playing what we may call an ordinary putt . . . I think it pays best in the long run to make a point of always hitting the ball with the middle of the face of the club.

~

The heart that does not quail when a yawning bunker lies far ahead of the tee just at the distance of a good drive, beats in trouble when there are but thirty inches of smooth, even turf to be run over before the play of the hole is ended.

~

The hole will never come to you; therefore make up your mind that you will always go to the hole, and let it be an invariable practice to play for the back of the tin so that you will always have just a little in hand.

Vardon was a private, rather modest man, but he certainly proved to be engaging using the written word. (Dale Concannon Collection at Phil Sheldon Golf Picture Library)

One of the greatest worries of the glorious life of old Tom Morris was that for a long time when in the middle of his career he was nearly always short with his long putts, and his son, young Tom, used wickedly to say that his father would be a great putter if the hole were always a yard nearer.

The old maxim "Never up, never in" is, I think, as valuable as ever . . . the man who is lacking in courage does not often win on the green. Nearly all good putters hit the ball with the utmost firmness.

ONCE I HIT UPON THE IDEA OF TRYING A PUTTER ABOUT A FOOT LONG. I TOOK IT OVER TO LA BOULIE TO USE IN THE FRENCH OPEN CHAMPIONSHIP, AND DID VERY WELL WITH IT FOR TWO ROUNDS. SO FAR AS I CAN RECOLLECT, I WAS LEADING VERY COMFORTABLY AT THE END OF THIRTY-SIX HOLES. EARLY IN THE THIRD ROUND I WAS PRESENTED WITH A PUTT OF NO MORE THAN SIX INCHES. MY RIGHT HAND JUMPED; I WENT ABOUT TWO FEET PAST THE HOLE, AND MY PARTNER, WHO WAS A FRENCHMAN, GAVE VENT TO A VERY DELIBERATE AND WHOLESOMELY ENGLISH—"GOOD HEAVENS!" I FINISHED THAT ROUND PUTTING WITH AN IRON, AND WITH A GOOD DEAL OF IRON IN MY SOUL.

I sometimes think that with putts of a yard or four feet, it would be best if, without more than a cursory look at the line, we were to walk up to the ball and unaffectedly knock it into the hole.

The bugbear of the short putt is, perhaps, that one is apt to exaggerate its difficulties.

I certainly do not believe in standing with the feet far apart. Rather I would go to the other extreme and have the heels touching.

I am a wholehearted believer in the overlapping grip for putting, and even the person who does not fancy it in driving can adapt himself easily to it on the green.

The fate of a short putt is an extreme; it is either perfect or ghastly. There is no mediocrity, no chance of recovery. That is why, I presume, the stroke is so trying; it is so fateful.

Vardon demonstrates his idea for a good stance and backswing on a long putt. He wrote: "(The back-swing) involves a very slight turn of the hips. The position of the arms produces the beginning of a pendulum swing." (From The Gist of Golf*)*

Now we see the finish of a long-putt swing. Vardon wrote: "The clubhead has followed through as nearly as possible on the line of the putt and has risen slightly from the ground." (From The Gist of Golf)

In nearly all cases, the missing of short putts is caused by the moving of the head.

I can generally putt better when I have to "borrow" some ground to allow for a slope than when the stroke is perfectly straightforward. The reason, I think, is that the sloping green makes the player ponder, whereas on a flat green he is prone to come to the conclusion that there is not much to consider. And concentration of the mind is the surest means to successful putting.

I do not believe in studying the line from its two ends. The player who examines the situation first from the ball and then from the hole is likely to see two lines. He finds himself filled with philosophic fears and speculative doubts. The harvest that he reaps is so rich that he is distracted by it. He borrows a bit from one line and a bit from the other, and finishes where Fortune and a baffling complexity of slopes may take him.

If the golfer will adjourn to a green to practice putting in the dusk of an evening, I feel sure that he will find the whole business much easier than it seems in the daytime. With light just sufficient to enable him to detect the dim outlines of the slopes, but not enough to give him the opportunity of exaggerating their horrors, he will discover himself putting with splendid self-reliance and success.

5 Strategy

Golf is made up of details, and it is the player who considers all the small points who succeeds in the end.

~

To the player who is in the throes of incapacity with a certain club, a new implement is ethereal; it holds out unbounded promise.

~

Don't play too much golf if you want to get on in the game. Three rounds a day are too much for any man, and if he makes a practice of playing them whenever he has the opportunity, his game is sure to suffer.

~

Do not wear too tightly fitting clothes. Particularly be careful to see that there is plenty of spare cloth under the arms.

Take care that there are plenty of nails [spikes] on the soles of your boots and shoes, and that they are in good condition and the heads not worn away. Nails in this state are almost useless, and create a great tendency towards slipping.

~

Unless you have a very good and special reason for doing so, do not play in gloves. The grip is seldom so secure and exact as when it is effected with the bare hands.

~

In wet weather it is a good thing to carry a piece of chalk in your pocket, and to rub the face of the driver and brassie with it each time before making a stroke. It prevents the ball from skidding.

~

Always use a clean ball, and carry [something] to keep it clean with.

~

It is one of the best of hints to carry two drivers. The frequency with which one will prove friendly when the other has become peevish is astonishing. The explanation is to be found, I think, in the theory that the difference in the whippiness operates in connection with the variations in the pace of the swing. None of us swing at just the same speed every day.

A large crowd enircles the green at the 1898 Open (that's the British Open in today's parlance), with Vardon somewhere among the contestants putting out at Prestwick in Scotland. (Dale Concannon Collection at Phil Sheldon Golf Picture Library)

Remember that the player who first settles down to the serious business of a hard match has the advantage.

At the beginning of a match, do not worry yourself with the idea that the result is likely to be against you. By reflecting thus upon the possibilities of defeat one often becomes too anxious and loses one's freedom of style.

Try, whenever possible, to make matches with opponents who are at least as good, if not better, than yourself. This will do your game more good than playing with an inferior player.

Remember that more matches are lost through carelessness at the beginning than through any other cause. Always make a point of trying to play the first hole as well as you have ever played a hole in your life.

Be sure of securing a comfortable stance on the teeing ground. It is the only place at which you have the right to choose a stance, and you may as well make the most of it. So hunt for a favorable spot on which to tee the ball.

When there is an out-of-bounds area to be taken into consideration, tee the ball as far from it as the limits of the teeing ground will allow.

A long drive is not by any means everything, and the young golfer should resist any inclination to strive for the 250-yard ball to the detriment or even the total neglect of other equally important, though perhaps less showy, considerations in the playing of a hole.

~

A golfer must never be morbid. If he can't school himself to think that he is going to make the best drive of his life, just when it is most wanted, he should try not to think of anything at all.

~

Always play from a low tee, except when the wind is behind you.

~

I think it would be best from every point of view if golfers played for the carry instead of for the run, and why I suggest that a long carry from the tee should be encouraged. *(Vardon estimated that the rubber-core ball added twenty to forty yards of roll for shots and golfers got into the habit of trying to pull low shots that would run well. He didn't think the rubber-core ball carried significantly farther than the gutta-percha.)*

~

Nowadays, by playing for the pulled shot, it is possible to get truly extraordinary distance. One often reads of record drives, but I am sure that dozens of the longest drives have never been measured. In the summer of 1911, when the ground was so favorable to the run, there must have been lots of shots of more than four hundred yards. I know that at the long hole at Totteridge, which measures 540 yards, I was regularly getting onto the green with a drive and niblick. A mashie for my second would have meant going too far. Players in other places were assuredly having similar experiences. It is all very good fun while it lasts, but it is not good practice for the pastime in its entirety.

~

I suppose that, for the indifferent performer, there is no experience more trying than that of playing a hole in the teeth of a strong wind. The ball never seems to go any distance, and . . . he often discovers that a topped shot which goes straight serves him as well as a properly struck ball. That is because the former dodges the wind, but as topping is not the proper game, it is obviously his duty to keep the ball as low as possible while making sure of raising it from the ground.

First of all, the tee should be low. The stance should be forward—with the hands the smallest distance conceivable in front of the ball during the address . . . for then, given a true swing, the club will come down on the ball in such a way as to keep it down throughout its flight.

Golf downwind is a simple business, as long as you pay sufficient prospective attention to the hazards ahead. The drive is easy; the chief danger is that of getting into a bunker which is meant to catch a bad second shot. In the absence of such peril, tee high (but not so high as to introduce the possibility of hitting under the ball), stand rather behind the ball, swing truly, and at the time of impact throw most of the weight on to the right leg so as to lift the ball into the air, and give it the full benefit of the wind.

In a powerful wind, the slice is easier to regulate than the pull . . . my advice to the golfer who desires to consistently conquer a turbulent air (and, incidentally, his opponent) is to pin his faith to the cut stroke.

Take more risks when you are down to an opponent than when you are up on him.

It is a mistake continually to exercise extreme caution. One's play is severely cramped by an excess of care.

Never hurry when playing a match or a medal round, or indeed any kind of golf. Haste will affect your nerves and spoil your play.

If you are playing golf in the afternoon, do not lunch any more heavily than you feel to be necessary.

Do not attempt to play two kinds of golf at the same time; that is to say, if you are playing for a medal, do not keep up a hole-to-hole match with your partner. You will become confused, with no clear idea of what you are trying to do, and you will probably win neither the medal nor the match.

"*Nil desperandum*" should always be the motto of the competition player, and it is a motto that will probably pay better in golf than in any other game.

It is very interesting to play on a course where one hardly ever has the same kind of stance for two shots in succession. A golfer who thinks can always adjust his stance to the situation; the chief points to remember are . . . to stand behind the ball for an uphill lie and forward for a hanging lie.

I know good golfers who say that when the ball is hanging—that is to say, resting on a downhill slope—you should stand rather more behind the ball than usual, with most of the weight on the right leg, and the body turned well towards the hole, so as to secure the effect of a cut shot . . . This may be all very well for a short shot with a mashie, but when it is necessary to hit a long shot with an iron, I believe in standing a trifle more forward than usual. In fact, it is a safe rule in all circumstances . . . When you stand a trifle in front, there is far less likelihood of hitting the turf behind the ball.

For an uphill lie, my own method is to stand a little more behind the ball than in the ordinary way, so as to avoid digging into the turf in front as the ball is hit.

Don't praise your own good shots. Leave that function to your partner, who, if a good sort, will not be slow in performing it. His praise will be more discriminating and worth more than yours.

When a hole is being keenly contested, and you look as though you are having the worst of it, try not to appear pleased when your opponent makes a bad stroke or gets into serious trouble, however relieved or even delighted you may feel.

Never lose your temper when you are in difficulties. Equanimity is half the battle.

The only thing to do when you see your ball disappear into an unpleasant place is to remember that many a hole is won when it looks lost beyond recall.

Sometimes, in a hazard, it is worth remembering that one is entitled to retrace one's steps; nobody likes it, but occasionally it is the easiest and safest way out of trouble, especially when there is a good chance of reaching the green with the next shot.

I have long since come to the conclusion that it is unwise to entertain any notion about performing heroics in hazards. The best thing to do is to look for the easiest way out, and take the line of least resistance.

We must fix our eye on a spot an inch and a half or two inches behind the ball, and determine to delve right into the bunker—as far into it as we can penetrate—with a forcible blow of the niblick. We shall need a full swing for the purpose. It can be as full a swing as for the drive, but it must be a considerably more upright one because we want to dig the ball out of its retreat. There should be no element of the sweeping action about this stroke.

The less distance you want to go, the more sand you take.

The sand—or even the harder stuff—if agitated in the right place, and with plenty of power, will nearly always release its victim.

I have very seldom seen soil so hard that it cannot be excavated, although sometimes a great amount of vigor is necessary. I shall never forget a wonderful shot which Joshua Taylor played in a distinctly clayey ditch at Clacton-on-Sea. He must have buried the head of his niblick nearly a foot below the surface, but the ball came out all right. Indeed, if I remember aright, he laid it dead.

If he is playing several more in a vain endeavor to extricate himself from a bunker, do not stand near him and audibly count his strokes. It would be justifiable homicide if he wound up his pitiable exhibition by applying his niblick to your head.

In some circumstances it is safer when playing a long shot up to the green to hug the wing hazards, and even get into one of them, than to send the ball straight up the middle and risk a lot of trouble beyond the hole.

In this connection, the peculiarities of the seventeenth—the famous "Road" hole—at St. Andrews at once occur to the mind. When the ground is hard, the ordinary game is to put the second shot at the foot of the slope in front of the green, run up, and hope for a four, while feeling satisfied to take five. But if you want to adopt bold tactics, it is better to go to the left in spite of the bunker that is there awaiting you, than to play straight and submit yourself to the danger of finishing on the dreaded road, whence in all probability you will simply return to the bunker. This latter hazard is an excellent one in which to execute a niblick-burying shot behind the ball. There is a good chance of getting dead from it, or sufficiently near the hole to obtain a four.

MOST OF US HAVE PAID THE PENALTY AT SOME TIME OR OTHER OF A VAULTING AMBITION TO DO SOMETHING WONDERFUL IN A BUNKER. MY UNHAPPIEST EXPERIENCE IN THIS RESPECT WAS IN A PROFESSIONAL TOURNAMENT AT MUSSELBURGH A GOOD MANY YEARS AGO. AT THE FOURTH HOLE, A SHORT ONE, I WAS BUNKERED NEAR THE GREEN. I TRIED TO PLAY A CLEVER SHOT OUT WITH MY MASHIE (VERY FOOLISHLY I CARRIED NO NIBLICK IN THOSE DAYS), WITH THE RESULT THAT I TOOK THREE SHOTS IN THE HAZARD. THEN I WENT ON TO BEACH, FROM WHICH PLACE I FOUND MY WAY BACK INTO THE BUNKER IN WHICH I HAD HAD ALL THE TROUBLE.

THE HOLE COST ME NINE, AND I SHALL NEVER FORGET THE LOOK OF WITHERING SCORN ON THE FACE OF MY CADDIE AS HE SAID WHEN THE BALL ULTIMATELY WENT DOWN: "YE'LL HAVE A NIBLICK THIS AFTERNOON, OR I'LL NO' CARRY FOR YE." DURING THE LUNCHEON INTERVAL HE WENT OFF TO OBTAIN A NIBLICK. HE CAME BACK EXCEEDINGLY INTOXICATED, BUT BEARING THE INSTRUMENT WHICH HE HAD SWORN TO MAKE ME USE. AS I WAS LUCKY ENOUGH TO WIN THE TOURNAMENT IN SPITE OF MY MORNING MISHAP, HE FELT WELL REPAID FOR HIS PAINS AND EVEN PERHAPS FOR HIS ACHING HEAD ON THE FOLLOWING MORNING.

When playing in frosty weather, do not take it for granted that because the greens are hard they are also fast.

~

Don't act upon the advice of your caddie when you are convinced in your own mind that he is wrong.

~

Golfers should, I think, sometimes be on their guard lest a too kind-hearted caddie, in an excess of zeal for his employer, should be tempted to transgress the laws of the game, or depart from strict truthfulness in his behalf. Sometimes it is done with a wonderful air of innocence and simplicity.

~

Always use the club that takes the least out of you . . . Never say, "Oh, I think I can reach it with such and such a club."

~

Do not be tempted to invest in a sample of each new golfing invention as soon as it makes its appearance. If you do, you will only complicate and spoil your game and encumber your locker with much useless rubbish.

6

Instruction and Practice

On almost every course one sees many people who are clear examples of early neglect.

For the beginner, there is no preparation so good as that of practicing for a month or two without playing so much as a single complete round.

In my early days as a professional, I devoted practically a year to practice.

For a beginner or foozler of long standing, nothing could be better than an hour's practice every day for a month and an entire abstinence from competitive rounds. I know that it is a lot to ask of a person who is longing to prove his progress and prowess by conquering somebody, but it is the surest means of economizing on the links in time and money that was ever conceived.

The main point is that this system of practicing without having to bother about an opponent's shot cultivates the gift of concentration, and enables the player to reflect upon the lessons that he has learned and to try and fathom the causes of his failure if he is not executing the strokes satisfactorily.

There are very few golfers devoid of ambition to make headway at the pastime, but undoubtedly there are many who feel that it would be a frittering away of time to take lessons, when they might be contesting some exciting games. The ease with which the ball can be persuaded a considerable distance has generated a spirit of heedlessness. This type of golfer is very unwise, because a short course of tuition at the outset of his golfing career might have been the means of giving him victory on numerous occasions when defeat has been his portion.

Possibly you have a golfing friend who may be even as good a golfer as your professional, but I say to you, listen to the expert with whom golf is a business rather than to the clever amateur to whom it is merely a diversion.

~

It has been said that there are ninety-nine things to remember while playing a stroke . . . I say that there are just two primary and all-important points to remember: They are to grip the club properly and to keep the head steady. Master those two difficulties, and you are certain to advance in some degree.

~

Enthusiasts have adopted truly noble and desperate measures in order to master this necessity (of keeping the head still during the swing). There was once a man who tied his head to a tree as a means of teaching it a lesson. Whenever it received a jerk—and some of the jerks must have been almost sufficient to dislocate his neck—he knew that he had committed the old error.

There was another player who thought of a highly ingenious device. I understand that to a button on his waistcoat he affixed a piece of elastic—not securely, but with just sufficient firmness that a real tug at it would pull it off the button. The other end he held tightly in his teeth so that the elastic was moderately taut without being severely stretched. Then he set his teeth with great purpose and made his swing. His theory was that if the elastic jumped off the button and smacked him in the face, he would know that he had moved his head. Unfortunately, he had forgotten that his body would move with his head.

The player who goes straight out and expects to put the hints into operation as though he had only to hear them in order to master them is not likely to profit greatly by his lessons. By the time he reaches the fourth hole, he forgets nearly everything in his anxiety to do something better than his opponent.

It has been my privilege to teach the first principles of the game to many [women], and I am bound to say that for the most part I have found them excellent pupils—better generally than the men learners. They seem to take closer and deeper notice of the hints you give them, and to retain the points of the lesson longer in their memories.

Many [women] somewhat spoil their prospects by concluding too hastily that they must play an altogether different game from that of their men friends, that they must have special clubs, special methods, and so forth. This is not the case. No doubt it is well for ladies to admit at once that they cannot drive as far as the men. But otherwise the man's game and the lady's game are the same in principle and in practice.

Success in approaching is largely a matter of practice—not of physical attributes nor an inborn capacity for playing games.

No matter what the grade of golfer, practice is valuable to him.

It is as easy to learn to play well as it is to learn to play badly. So I advise every golfer to get hold of the game stroke by stroke, and never be too ambitious at the commencement.

No matter what the grade of golfer, practice is valuable to him. Never can he be so good a player that it is impossible for him to be better. Personally, I have made it a rule to practice "on my own" at frequent intervals all my life, and I am certain that every successful golfer has done the same. Man for man, or woman for woman, there is infinitely more devotion to this subject among advanced players than there is where the less-accomplished performers are concerned. That is precisely why the former are advanced. The trouble is to make the less accomplished appreciate the importance of a lonely hour on the links.

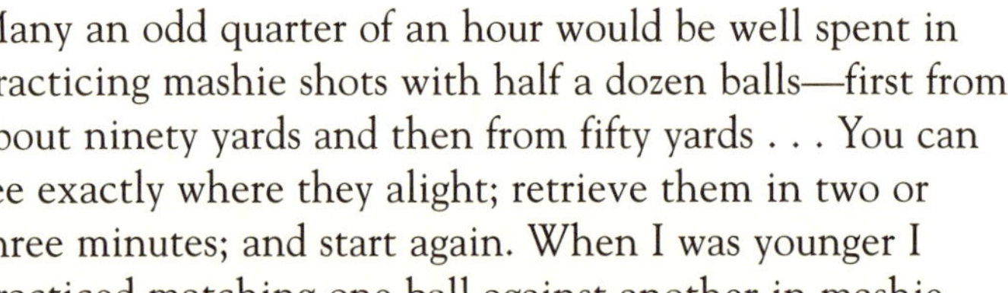

Many an odd quarter of an hour would be well spent in practicing mashie shots with half a dozen balls—first from about ninety yards and then from fifty yards . . . You can see exactly where they alight; retrieve them in two or three minutes; and start again. When I was younger I practiced matching one ball against another in mashie pitches. It taught my hand and eye a lot.

A young Vardon swinging away. (Dale Concannon Collection at Phil Sheldon Golf Picture Library)

When practicing, use the club that gives you the most trouble, and do not waste your time in knocking a ball about with the tool that gives you the most satisfaction and with which you rarely make a bad stroke.

~

For the player who desires to advance, I recommend at least three hours' practice every week. And in the interests of the golfing community, it may be suggested that these outings should have their base somewhere near the edge of the fairway instead of in the middle. They are apt to result in the lifting of a good many divots, some of them very large if the player is in his novitiate.

~

I once saw a beginner at Totteridge miss the ball completely and yet lose it. He slogged blindly with an iron and lifted a piece of turf about as big as a soup plate. The divot dropped neatly on the ball just in front. Not seeing the latter object, the player thought he had hit it. "Where's it gone?" he asked excitedly. It was not until somebody told him to replace the divot that he found it had not gone at all.

There is no harm occasionally in playing a hole on your own. What I used to do frequently was to take a couple of balls and play them against one another . . . There is really quite a lot of fun in it, with the added recommendation of usefulness. You concentrate equally on the shots since it is not a matter of being beaten by somebody, and at each hole you get two drives, two irons or pitches, and all the putts that fate may prompt you to take.

I used to play nine holes in this way, and I found that if I got two or three up on myself, the resolution with which my worse half would set about the task of retrieving the situation was such as to keep me intensely interested all the time.

Putting practice on undulating greens is very valuable, not so much because it teaches the golfer exactly what allowance he should make in various cases, but because it helps by experience to give him the courage of his convictions.

~

I have never in my life taken a single golfing lesson from anyone, and that whatever style I may possess is purely the result of watching others play and copying them when I thought they made a stroke in a particularly easy and satisfactory manner.

~

7

The Golf Course, Etiquette, and Assorted Mulligans

THE GOLF COURSE

My idea of a good course for modern golf is . . . it should make the player revert to the old desire to obtain the longest possible carry from the tee, and then he will soon discover how to play the lofted approach with an iron club—the shot which has almost disappeared from the game, and the disappearance of which has done so much to lower the standard of play.

~

In modern golf, no holes are harder to play than the short ones, provided that they are properly designed . . . Whatever facilities the ball may afford at the long holes, it is certain that it cannot help anybody at the short ones, and so the latter tend to restore some of the demand for the skill. They must, however, call for perfect tee shots. There must be no mercy for the errant player.

~

The diagonal bunker comes into use at the longer holes. Of these, the hardest to play under modern conditions are, I think, those which measure about four hundred yards, and have well-protected greens . . . I firmly believe in having a bunker in front of the green with the object of making the golfer play for the carry, which is the true game; but the hazard should be about forty yards short of the pin. In dry weather it is often well-nigh impossible to make the ball stop within a few yards of where it alights.

Except at short holes, or where short approaches constituted the natural sequence to good drives, I would have the back of the green guarded only at a respectful distance—say, from ten to fifteen yards beyond the hole. It is a good thing to tempt a player to go boldly for the pin, and he is apt to become frightened (and reasonably so) when he knows that the slightest excess of courage may bring irretrievable disaster upon his head.

It is a great compliment to pay to a course to say that it encourages bold approaching. The green which is closely hemmed on all sides by bunkers and which, in the distance, looks hardly big enough to accommodate a foursome, may inspire skillful iron play in some instances, but it is much more likely to generate a spirit of timidity among golfers.

Pot bunkers scattered here and there just off the line are good, because they exercise an extraordinary magnetism on the golfer, and it should be his duty to overcome that influence.

There is much to be said for grassy hazards—punishing places of much the same size and shape as bunkers, but with rough ground instead of sand as the fundamental feature. Rough is harder to get out of than sand.

There is no end to the tricks and difficulties of a good sporting green, and the more of them the merrier. The golfer's powers of calculation are now in great demand.

IF WE COULD TAKE A POND ON A COURSE AND ANY BUNKER OF EQUAL SIZE, AND COUNT THE NUMBER OF SHOTS HIT INTO EACH IN A YEAR, WE SHOULD ALMOST ASSUREDLY FIND THE POND AN EASY WINNER. BY NO MEANS IS THIS MYSTERIOUS ATTRACTIVE POWER OF WATER PECULIAR TO GOLF. IT IS IN THE NATURE OF THINGS FOR PEOPLE TO BE DRAWN TOWARD WATER (EXCEPT, POSSIBLY, AS A BEVERAGE); THAT IS WHY THEY WALK TO THE EDGE OF A LAKE TO INSPECT IT WHEN THEY WOULD HAVE JUST AS GOOD A VIEW FROM A DISTANCE OF THIRTY YARDS AND WHY THEY STAND ON A BRIDGE OR AN EMBANKMENT GAZING INTO A RIVER AND YET LOOKING AT NOTHING IN PARTICULAR—EXCEPT WATER.

BUT THIS FASCINATION IS THE STRONGER IN GOLF BECAUSE, EVEN WHILE THE VISION IS FOCUSED ON THE BALL JUST BEFORE THE STROKE, THE POND STILL LIVES IN THE MIND'S EYE. IT IS SOMETHING TO BE AVOIDED, BUT THE PICTURE OF IT IS THERE ALL THE WHILE, EXERCISING A STRANGE ALLUREMENT.

IF PROOF WERE NEEDED OF THE EXISTENCE OF THIS INFLUENCE, IT COULD BE FOUND IN THE NOVEL RECORD WHICH HAS BEEN ESTABLISHED AT GARDEN CITY, NEW YORK—THE CLUB

THAT IS UPPERMOST IN THE MINDS OF BRITISHERS WHEN THEY THINK OF AMERICAN GOLF, BY REASON OF THE FACT THAT MR. W. J. TRAVIS, PLAYING AS ITS REPRESENTATIVE, TOOK THE BRITISH AMATEUR CHAMPIONSHIP CUP TO REPOSE UNDER ITS ROOF IN 1904. GARDEN CITY HAS—OR HAD—A POND AT ITS LAST HOLE, AND I UNDERSTAND THAT CLUB STATISTICIANS HAVE CALCULATED THE NUMBER OF BALLS THAT ENTER ITS CLUTCHES IN A YEAR. THEY PUT THE LOSS DOWN AT FIVE THOUSAND BALLS IN TWELVE MONTHS.

A SUGGESTION HAS BEEN MADE, I GATHER, THAT A NET SHOULD BE LAID AT THE BOTTOM OF THE POND AND DRAWN UP PERIODICALLY SO AS TO RECOVER THE TREASURE. TRAWLING MIGHT BE A GOOD SOLUTION TO THE PROBLEM, BUT IT IS MERELY A MATTER OF FURTHER ARITHMETICAL WORK TO DECIDE HOW LONG IT WILL TAKE TO FILL THE POND COMPLETELY WITH BALLS, AND THUS PREVENT ANY OTHERS FROM BEING SUNK. THE PLAYER WOULD THEN SIMPLY WALK ON TO THE EXPANSE OF RUBBER-CORED PEBBLES, AND PLAY HIS BALL WHERE IT LAY—IF HE COULD DISTINGUISH IT.

I consider the links of the Royal St. George's Club to be the best that are to be found anywhere. There is, in the first place, not a single tee shot in the round where good play must not be shown by the golfer if he wants to achieve success.

~

I call St. Andrews a good course generally; but its bunkers are badly placed. They punish the man who is driving well more than the man who is driving badly, for they are generally the length of a good long drive.

~

For some reasons I like Muirfield; but it does not enjoy so many advantages as the other championship courses. There are not so many sandhills. It is on the flat side, and at first glance you might take it to be an inland course.

~

ETIQUETTE

Obtain a thorough knowledge of the rules of the game, always play strictly according to them, and adhere rigidly to the etiquette of golf.

Make a point of seeing that your caddie always replaces your divots, or replace them yourself if you have no caddie. This, as we all know, is a golfer's first duty.

Be careful that you always stand on the proper side of the tee when your opponent is preparing to drive.

Always fill in afterwards each hole that you make in a bunker.

Never try your shots over again when there are other players behind you.

If from any cause you are playing a very slow game, don't miss an opportunity of inviting the couple behind you to pass. It will please them, and will be far more comfortable for you. But if your match is behind a slow one, do not be offensive in pressing upon the match in front by making rude remarks and occasionally playing when they are in range.

Never practice swinging on the putting green.

In playing through the green, avoid as far as possible getting in your opponent's line of sight when he is making his stroke.

When carrying your own clubs, do not throw the bag down on the greens.

If you have no caddie, do not order your opponent's caddie about as if you were paying for his services.

ASSORTED MULLIGANS

I do not believe the man who says he plays only for exercise, and that he does not care whether his form is good or bad. As a rule, he makes such a remark when he is about five down at the turn.

Vardon enjoying what apparently is a relaxing round of golf. (Dale Concannon Collection at the Phil Sheldon Golf Library)

IT IS A PITY THAT THE WORLD OF CADDYING IS NOT FULL OF ZEALOTS WITH TONGUES SO CAUSTIC AS THAT OF A MAN WHOM I ONCE HEARD ADDRESSING HIS EMPLOYER ON A LONDON COURSE.

"DID I HEAR YOU SAY YOU CAME FROM AUSTRALIA?" HE ASKED OF THE PLAYER, WHO HAD HOWKED UP ABOUT A DOZEN HUGE DIVOTS IN A FEW HOLES.

"YES," WAS THE REPLY. "I'M FROM DOWN UNDER."

"WELL, SAID THE CADDIE, "IF YOU GO ON LIKE THIS, YOU'LL SOON BE HOME."

~

The ignorant caddie is trying, but not less is the one who knows too much about the game, or thinks he does, and insists upon inflicting his superior knowledge upon you during the whole course of the round.

~

Whether you wear boots or shoes should be governed in a large degree by the extent to which you use your ankles when playing. Braid and Taylor always play in boots. Personally, I prefer shoes: I make a lot of use of my ankles, and like them free. In any case, very thick soles are bad.

Collars are by no means unimportant details of dress. It is as well to have something around your neck for appearance's sake, but it is bad when that something stands two inches or more in height. I can assure the reader that most of the professionals have their collars specially made for them. They are an inch high. I mean, of course, that the collars are an inch high—not the professionals.

I have nothing to say on the burning question of trousers versus knickerbockers, except that the latter facilitate that freedom of the ankle and leg which is so desirable. I have no particular pattern of tie to suggest; in fact, I am finished with the subject of clubs and clothes.

Home exercises of the dumb-bell and Indian club variety, such as a good many golfers make a habit of performing with a view to strengthening their arms and wrists, are not necessary. Indeed, sometimes they are positively harmful from a golfing point of view, since they may develop strength of muscle as opposed to what I would call a healthy and normal suppleness.

Bibliography

Material used and excerpted in this book was drawn from the following books, all authored by Harry Vardon:

Golf Club Selection. Newark, Ohio: The Burke Golf Company, 1916.

How to Play Golf. London: Methuen and Co., 1912.

Success at Golf. Boston: Little, Brown, and Co., 1914.

Progressive Golf. Toronto: McClelland and Stewart Publishers, 1922.

The Complete Golfer. London: Methuen and Co., 1905.

The Gist of Golf. New York: George H. Doran Co., 1922.